I0867421

EARTH IN DANGER

FUTURE ENERGY

By Emily Kington

Words that appear in **BOLD** are explained in the glossary.

First published by Hungry Tomato Ltd in 2022
F1, Old Bakery Studios, Blewetts wharf, Malpas Road, Truro, Cornwall, TR1 1QH, UK.

Copyright © Bright Bound Ltd 2022

www.hungrytomato.com
All rights reserved. No part of this work may be reproduced or utilized in any form or by any means, electronic or mechanical, including photocopying, recording or by any information storage and retrieval system, without the prior written permission of the publisher.

ISBN 978-1-914087-42-4

A CIP catalog record for this book is available from the British Library

Manufactured in the USA

Picture credits (t=top, b=bottom, m=middle, l-left, r=right, bg=background)

Science photo library: 13br; 16bl. **Getty Images:** 25t. **Shutterstock**: Sungsu han 23-24bg, 26mr; Jaroslava V 3bg; 5tr; 7tl; 7tr; 8br; Jenson 14-15bg; 14bl; Vlastas 16-17bg; VectorMine 18tl; Creative Travel projects 18-19bg; 19br; Natascha Kaurorat 20-21bg; Tchara 21br; Mis_uma 24ml; nEwyyy 24br; 25bl; Rawpixel.com 25br; Rawpixel.com 26br; 26mr; Sergey Tinyakov 27ml; Denis Belitsky 27tr; Olga Danylenko 27b; 28tl; 28br; Olivier Le Moal 29br; Nimur 29tr; Studio Harmony 29ml; Daisy Daisy 30bl; Rawpixel.com 30tr; 32br; Nana44 1bg, 31bg; Susan Santa Maria 4-5bg; 6-7bg; Petrmalinak 2bg, 8-9bg; 10-11bg; Max Topchii 12-13bg.

Every effort has been made to trace the copyright holders, and we apologize in advance for any unintentional omissions. We would be pleased to insert the appropriate acknowledgements in any subsequent edition of this publication.

CONTENTS

People can't live without energy. We need it for food, heat, light and transport. We also need it to power our homes and businesses.

A lot of the energy we use comes from burning coal, oil and gas. We call these **fossil fuels**.

Using fossils fuels is damaging our planet and causing our **climate** to change. They are also running out!

DID YOU KNOW?

Fossil fuels are made from the remains of plants and animals that died millions of years ago.

THE ENERGY PROBLEM

Oil rigs drill for fuel deep underground. Some stand on stilts in the ocean.

Most of the energy we use is made from non-renewable resources, such as oil, natural gases and coal. They are being used up faster than they can be replaced.

When fossil fuels are burned, they release gases, such as carbon dioxide, that can pollute the **environment**.

Too much carbon dioxide in the **atmosphere** can cause too much heat to stay trapped on Earth. This is making our planet warmer. This could seriously affect all life on Earth.

We need to find different ways to make energy.

A coal burning power station releasing carbon dioxide.

NON-RENEWABLE ENERGY

Burning gas

Burning coal

Some types of energy are produced from renewable resources. This means that they won't run out over time.

Renewable energy can be produced from:

- Solar from the Sun (Solar Power).
- The wind (Wind Power).
- Movement of water from **tides** and water rushing down hill (Hydroelectric Power).
- Heat and steam produced underground (Geothermal Power).

Not only are these energy sources renewable, they are also better for the planet.

Ocean waves can also be used to make energy (Wave Power).

RENEWABLE ENERGY

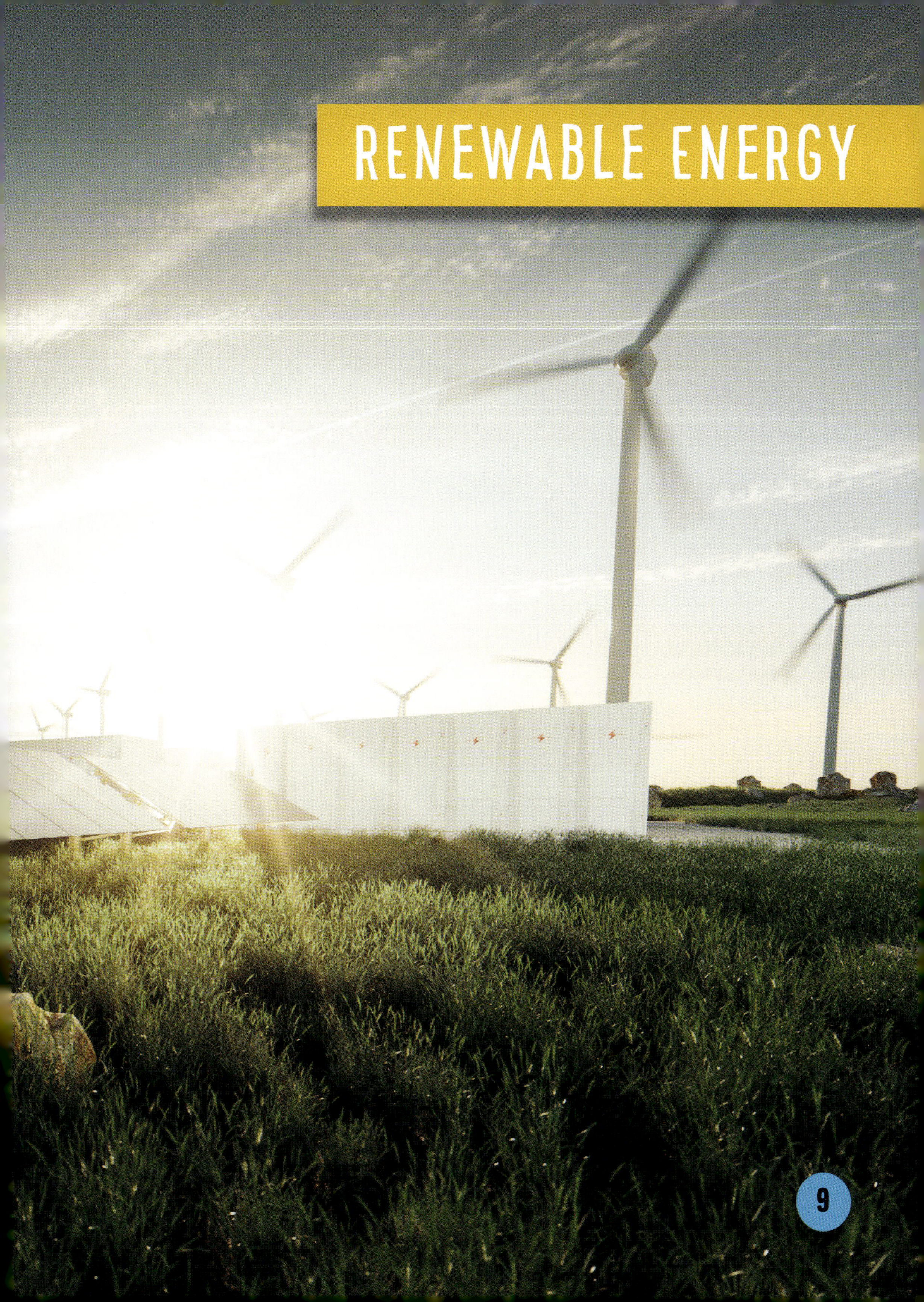

WHAT IS CLEAN ENERGY?

This machine uses solar energy to heat water.

'Clean' energy produces very little, or no polluting gases, such as carbon dioxide.

One way to make cleaner energy is to change how we burn fossil fuels, so that they don't give off lots of gas.

An even better solution is to stop using fossil fuels altogether, and switch to renewable sources that make clean energy. However, some types of renewable energy can be harmful to the planet in the process of being made and transported.

DID YOU KNOW?

The force of river water pouring through a **dam** can make lots of clean electricity, but it could also harm the **habitats** of many plants and animals.

WIND & WATER POWER

Wind turbines standing in the ocean.

Movement created by wind and water can be used to produce clean, renewable energy.

Wind power is created using **wind turbines**. The propeller-like blades on a turbine are turned by the wind. The turning blades cause a **generator** to spin, which creates electricity.

For hydroelectric power, tides in the ocean, rivers, or water released from a dam, are used to turn large, underwater turbines, which create energy.

A tidal power station where the fast-flowing water is used to produce electricity.

The Sun is Earth's biggest energy source. It naturally produces heat and light, which we use every day.

We are able to turn sunlight directly into energy, using **solar panels.**

Solar panels are made of individual cells, which trap sunlight and turn it into electrical energy. They can also be used to heat up water.

In the future, it may be possible to put big solar panels into space and send the power down to Earth.

Many people now have solar panels on their roof to help power their home.

DID YOU KNOW?

Satellites in space already use solar panels to power themselves.

SOLAR POWER

Solar power stations trap sunlight to bring power to homes and businesses.

Nuclear power stations use nuclear energy to produce electricity.

Nuclear energy is released from chemicals, like **uranium**. This process uses a lot of water, but it doesn't make any carbon dioxide, or other harmful gases.

However, there are problems with nuclear power. The stations are expensive to build and run. They also produce small amounts of dangerous waste that can be very harmful to living things if not kept secure. Scientists are working on new types of nuclear power that may solve these problems.

Uranium is **mined** from deep underground. There may not be enough uranium in the world to keep stations working in the future.

NUCLEAR POWER

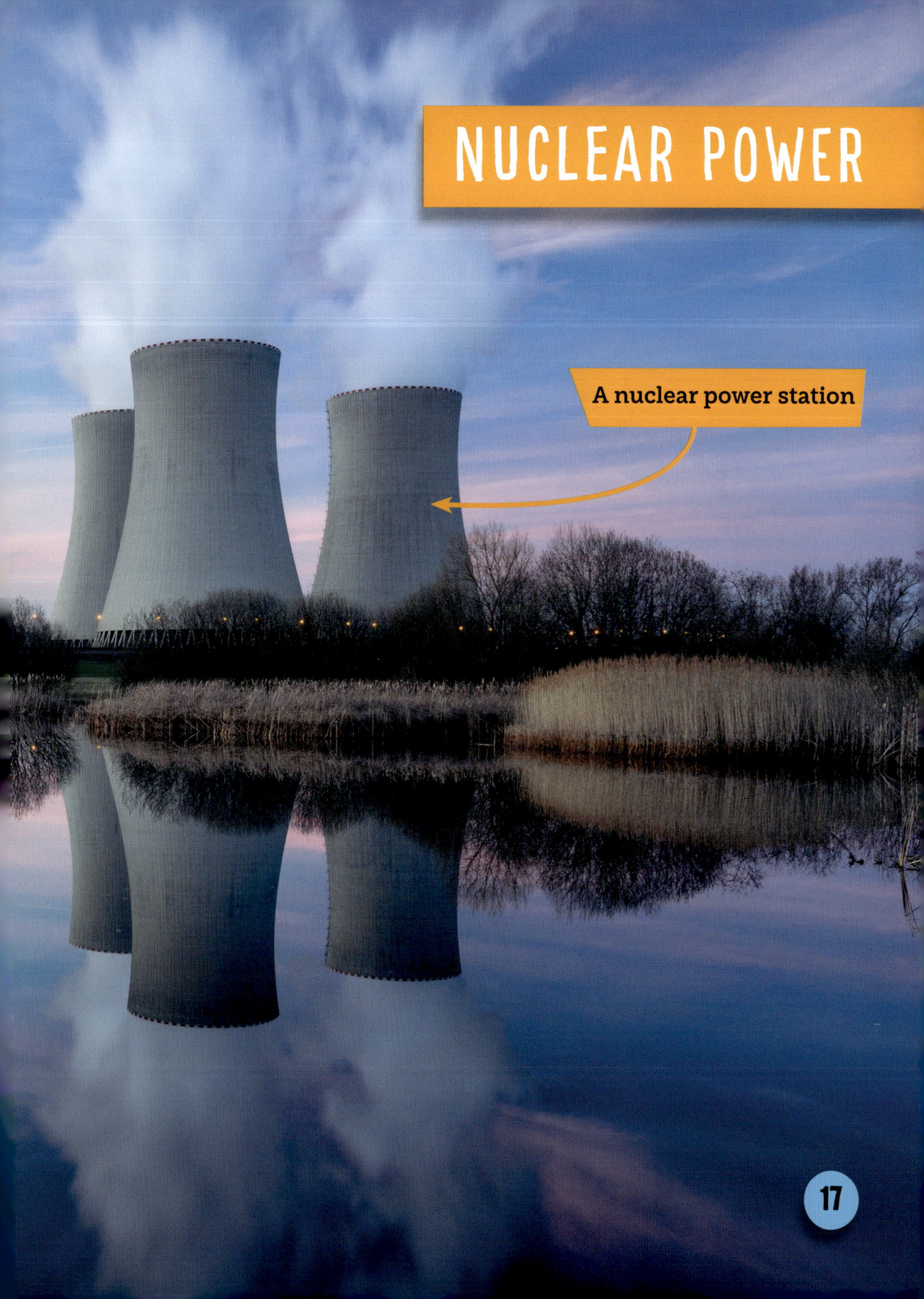

GEOTHERMAL ENERGY

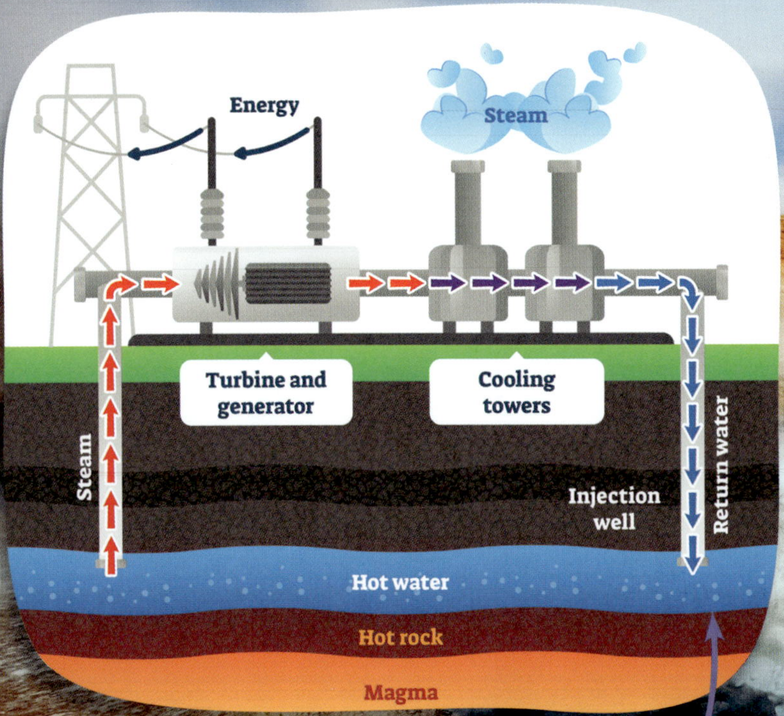

Diagram of how geothermal energy is produced.

Geothermal power comes from using the heat of the Earth itself.

This heat, in the form of hot water and steam, is often found in areas of volcanic activity.

With pipes and pumps, the water or steam is taken from deep underground. It is used to power turbines that then generate electricity.

Although geothermal energy is renewable, there are not many places in the world where it can be produced.

A geothermal power station

BIOMASS ENERGY

DID YOU KNOW?

Biomass can be very smelly, which is bad news if you live near where it is produced!

Biomass is used to create a renewable form of energy, but not a very clean one!

Biomass includes plants, such as corn, trees and sugar cane. It can also be made out of waste from humans, plants and animals, such as sawdust, grass clippings, animal manure, and even our food waste.

To create energy from it, biomass is usually burned. Burning it releases carbon dioxide into the air, which can speed up climate change.

Fuel for cars, buses and trucks mainly comes from oil. Oil is a fossil fuel, which won't last forever. It also causes pollution.

Electric cars do not produce harmful gases and are very quiet. Using them would make our cities much cleaner and quieter places. They run from electricity stored in big rechargeable batteries.

The energy needed to power electric cars needs to come from renewable sources in order to really cut back on using fossil fuels.

DID YOU KNOW?

Hybrid cars are powered by both oil and electricity. They use less fuel than normal cars, and can charge their batteries as they drive.

ELECTRIC & HYBRID CARS

An electric car charging station

FACT FILE

SAVING ENERGY

The best way to save energy, and help the environment, is to use less of it. Here are some ways that people can start saving energy.

TOP TIPS TO SAVE ENERGY:

- Wear more layers of clothing so you can turn down the heating.
- Close your curtains at night to keep the heat in.

- Switch off the lights when you leave a room.
- When you've finished watching TV or using the computer, turn them off. Don't leave them on standby.

- Use low-energy light bulbs.
- Hang your washing out to dry instead of using a dryer.
- Re-use or recycle materials.

FACT FILE

MOVING FORWARD: VEHICLES

Our roads are full of cars and other vehicles. In the USA, there are more than 270 million road vehicles in use!

- Using more electric vehicles could massively reduce the amount of fossil fuels we use.

- Walking, cycling or using public transport are much better for the environment than cars.
- Eating locally grown food cuts the number of trucks needed to transport food.

- Trains create less carbon dioxide than either cars or planes, and some are even powered by electricity.
- Planes produce more carbon dioxide than any other form of transport.

- Plan vacations closer to home so you don't need to fly.

FACT FILE

MAKING YOUR OWN ELECTRICITY

Houses are becoming more energy efficient. Some houses can even make their own electricity or heating.

SMALL WIND TURBINES

Small wind turbines can make electricity whenever the wind is blowing.

SOLAR PANELS

Solar panels can be fixed to a roof. The energy they generate can be stored and used even when the Sun isn't shining.

AIR SOURCE HEAT PUMPS

Air source heat pumps absorb heat from the air outside and use it to create heating and hot water for your home. They work a bit like a backwards refrigerator!

GROUND SOURCE HEAT PUMPS

Ground source heat pumps work in a similar way, but they absorb heat from underground, through a system of pipes.

Both types of heat pump need electricity to run, but are more energy efficient than regular heating systems.

HOW YOU CAN HELP

Here are some great projects to help save energy. Use the energy saving tips on pages 24-25 to help you.

SCHOOL PROJECT

Do an energy check and make a list of all of the ways your school could save energy and then talk to your teachers about putting your list into action!

GET COMPETITIVE!

Create a chart with columns for each member of your family. Every time someone does something to save energy, note it in their column. Who will be the energy saving champion?

GLOSSARY

atmosphere The thick layer of air that surrounds the Earth.

climate Patterns of weather over a long period of time.

dam A barrier that blocks the flow of water or sends it in a new direction.

energy efficient Using the smallest amount of natural resources possible to make energy, and to prevent energy loss.

environment An area or place where people, plants, and animals live.

fossil fuels Fuels, such as gas, oil and coal, made from living things that died millions of years ago.

generator A machine that produces electricity.

habitats A place where an animal or plant lives.

mined Removed from deep in the Earth.

non-renewable Produced from resources that will eventually run out, like coal or oil.

pollution Unwanted chemicals and other substances that harm the air, water, or land.

renewable Something that can be replaced and won't run out.

solar panels A device that traps energy from the Sun and changes it into electrical power.

tides The natural rising and falling of the sea level every day.

uranium A metal found deep underground that can be used in producing nuclear energy.

wind turbines Machines that turn the power of the wind into electricity.

INDEX